the neighborhood!

By

Jerry Van Amerongen

SIMON AND SCHUSTER
New York

Published by Simon and Schuster
A Division of Simon & Schuster, Inc.
Simon & Schuster Building
Rockefeller Center
1230 Avenue of the Americas
New York, New York 10020
SIMON AND SCHUSTER and colophon are registered trademarks of Simon & Schuster, Inc.

THE NEIGHBORHOOD™ is a trademark of The Register and Tribune
Syndicate, Inc., 715 Locust Street, Des Moines, Iowa 50309

Manufactured in the United States of America

10 9 8 7 6 5 4 3 2 1

Library of Congress Cataloging in Publication Data
Van Amerongen, Jerry.
   The neighborhood.
   1. Neighborhood—Caricatures and cartoons.
2. American wit and humor, Pictorial. I. Title.
NC1429.V34A4 1984   741.5'973   84-10629
ISBN 0-671-52322-8

"This could be trouble, Merle! . . ."

Luckless Capt. Zot and his alien force (disguised as lizards) are destroyed by a little known Midwestern fraternity.

"Helen, the dog wants in!"

"My brother, Tilford, had trouble with
hemorrhoids and he never did anything like this!"

In the spring of 1886, cowboy designer Yancy Pendleton introduced genuine chicken-hide boots . . . Thankfully they never caught on.

"Ben, you know it annoys me when you don't answer! . . ."

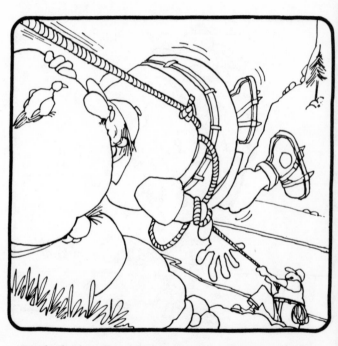

Rock climber Fred Belding enjoyed being the first one up the cliff or the last one up the cliff, but never the middle one up the cliff.

Biffy's bark is worse than his bite.

The annual blessing of the bedsprings:
another part of the glue that keeps
this neighborhood so close-knit.

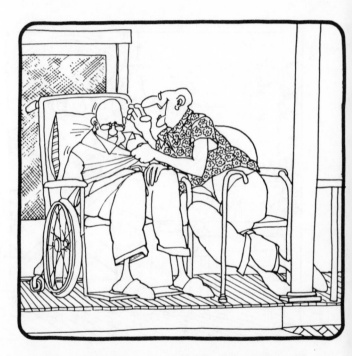

"I've got it, Bernie . . . I finally figured it out! . . .
I understand women, Bernie!"

Bill Angsley realized his wife was still smarting over last night's gin game when he found his breakfast stapled to a paper plate.

You can say what you like . . . but the Hensley Bros. move a lot of fruit.

Beginning next year, officials of the Miss Gurkey County pageant will more closely scrutinize the talent of prospective contestants.

"I see you still have your fever . . ."

Businessman lighting a cigarette in the wind.

"Ladies and gentlemen, Mr. Bolt Upright!"

This wasn't exactly what Ben had in mind.

While stuffed birds make striking hood ornaments, they become impractical at speeds above 55 mph.

"I'd like to get my hands on the guy who turned that phony rubber shark loose."

"Good afternoon, fellow workers!! . . ."

Near the end of 1st period, substitute teacher
Brenda Angsley was confronted with the
undeniable fact that this was
a tough school.

Although outwardly placid, this neighborhood
conceals a hotbed of Spider-People activity.

"Joan, I think I just caught my second wind! . . ."

"Leverage, Whithers! I haven't thought of leverage for years!"

Uncle Edwin makes his money contracting with banks to draw all but the tiniest amount of ink from their courtesy pens.

It was disconcerting to Professor Murray that James insisted upon dressing up for voice lessons.

"Brian, Cynthia! It's me, Dr. Larry Chandler! Something's gone terribly wrong!"

The taking of a three-way table lamp at 2117 Penn Ave. South.

The Incredible Hulk feeds his dog, Snyder.

"Fred . . . I told you to get the screens fixed!!"

"Thank you very much ladies and gentlemen! And now we'd like to do a Pink Floyd medley. . . ."

It's all Al can do to give life the benefit of the doubt.

"You've gotta use longer nails, Ann! . . ."

Tension mounted as Brad Dorsey rode the elevator to the 47th floor disguised as a mallard duck.

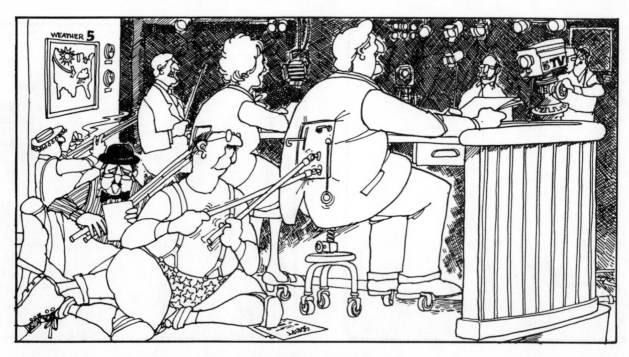

The truth about the 10 p.m. news.

Once again Elliot Zambini's tidiness ruins the act.

Bob's house is so isolated that he's taken
to communicating with passing cars.

This isn't gonna be one of Biffy
the lap dog's better days.

Ironically, it was young Greg Walcraft's blind acceptance of his business school's advice to "dress like your boss" that cost him further opportunities within the corporation.

Always mindful of others, Arthur tilts the desk blotter so his boss might better view his resignation letter.

"What a great sock collection, Farnley! How do you come by all these socks?! . . ."

An errant tennis ball and an unfortunate yawn conspired to keep Spot off solid foods for a few days.

Fred Pincer has a habit of rubbing people
the wrong way.

"THE BUSINESSMEN ARE COMING! THE
BUSINESSMEN ARE COMING!"

"Good lord, Berlingham, any one of us could have mistaken this for a costume ball! . . ."

Leo's hand/eye coordination caused him
a good deal of difficulty on his new job.

Professor Gurnsey shows us that a steady diet of
solid chocolate fishys will cause a cat to lose feeling
in its extremities.

"No more plum pudding for Mrs. Giddings . . ."

Let's talk
pipe fittings-
- HAVE A GLASS
of LEMONADE
.75¢

Feeling lightheaded while teaching his
dog to sneeze, Blaine takes a break.

The hazards of leadership.

"Careful, Dear . . . the Evening Grosbeak is loose! . . ."

Once on the gravel roof, building inspector Grayson realized he would have to cite this contractor for improperly bonding the stones.

This is the photo that pretty much closed the
Glenn Archer School of Retriever Training.

Carl encounters fear and its
unusual side effects.

Mrs. Gilpie's cat moved cautiously
along the clothesline.

Lamont had a very strict upbringing.

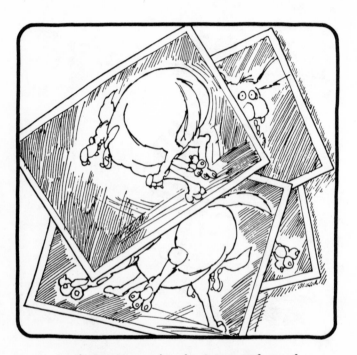

Lyle Biggs uses his dog's innate fear of flash photography to exercise his pet.

"Ethel! You'd better come see about the cat! . . ."

"Clifton, are we going to do this every time you catch your limit?!..."

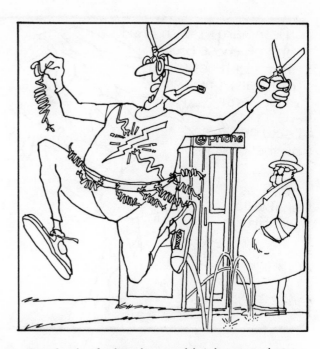

Ray had a feeling he wouldn't be completing his call at this particular time.

Susan returns the revised revision of Mr. Biggs'
latest rush project.

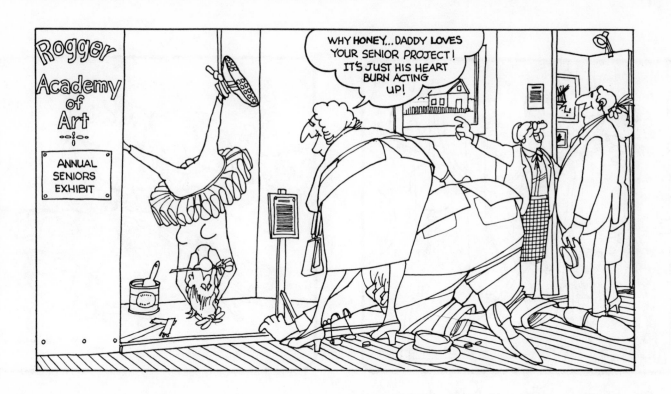

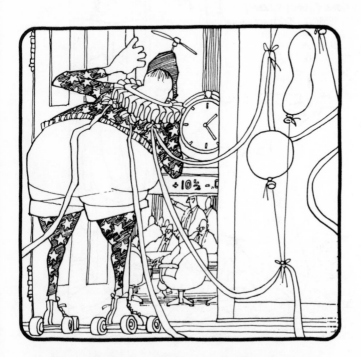

Glenn Trotter, just before he lost his clout as
a high-powered Wall Street analyst.

It was the German, Carl Klause, who brought a sense of engineering to the annual Writing Legibly With The Tiniest Pencil Contest.

retrospect, Marshall's decision to come to a complete stop at that particular intersection was a mistake."

"I'm gonna like this new kid," thought General Manager Glenn Habner.

The Doberman threw himself out the second-story window soon after he realized the family had indeed named him "Binky."

It's only a matter of time. . . .

Having an apartment below Freddie's Polka Palace limited Carl's spiritual growth.

Arnold Flackner has a small but enthusiastic following.

"You see, Wendell, that *was* your
scarf in the bus door! . . ."

About two miles into the portage, Professor
Bob ceased to be a positive factor.

"No wonder you've lost your nose for pheasant! . . ."

"Look, Spider . . . you gotta take a little torque off the ball on the short passing game."

Nobody in the Earl Greebey family knows
anything about gravity.

"For heaven's sake, Ned, how was he supposed to know those were your good shoes?"

Editor Wally Dickerson receives another letter from a concerned reader.

Store owner Artie Brodrick could see the sign already. In big red letters, it would read "No Loose Devices In The Store."

A moment's indecision at the elevator cost
Brian another suit.

"OK, Roger! Put the hair dryer away! . . ."

Late last night Sterling discovered his
brother-in-law owned a cat.

"Well, fight fans . . . young Rocky Slocum came to fight, make no mistake about that! . . ."

"How long have you been a nurse, Miss Dugen? . . ."

Skipper's beginning to have trouble
with his sense of smell.

The saga of Harold (Hard Luck) Hadley continues.

"Sid, you seem to be plunging along
a broad front. . . ."

Candidate Dimmer's habitual speaking gesture costs
him two more votes.

"Rudy! You found the short!"

Brad was sorry now that he asked Helen's
father to play the spoons.

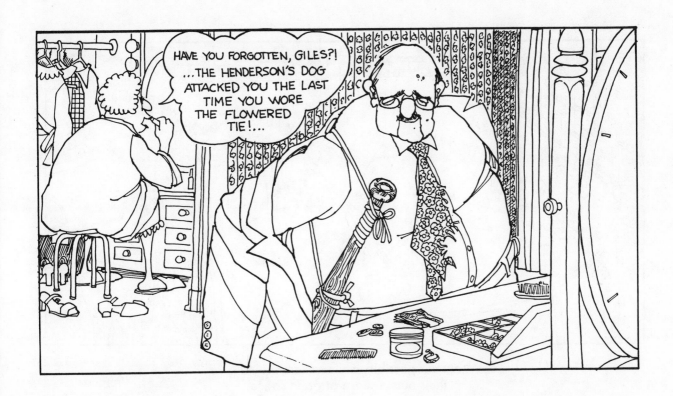

Whenever possible, city dwellers should give
their pets a sense of open space.

Sid Baldwin continues to be nagged by
a short attention span.

Meter reader Sal Pinko waits until everyone leaves so he can experience the thrill of sticking yet another "Sorry we missed you" card in the door.

"They're a lot of company, aren't they? . . ."

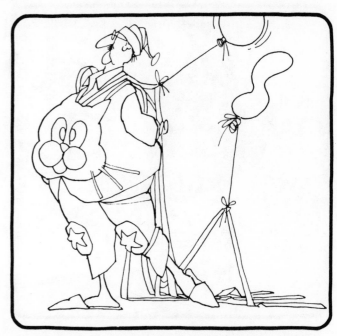

The idea for Edward's pajamas was revealed to him in a dream.

"Here's Howard now . . . oh, and Skipper too!"

On weekends Uncle Carl and Aunt Emma traveled to small
towns, where they masqueraded as Naval Reservists.

Carl's wife offers him proof that, yes, she was planning to serve "that stupid stringy Italian stuff" again.

Marilyn inadvertently uses the lint brush.

"Pardon me, I couldn't help but notice you're being bothered by a fly."

Lodge owner Harold Shuffle saw only the negative side of things.

Skipper sensed there were those who wished to
have him believe it was night . . . But why?! . . .

Due in large part to a steady diet of outdoor magazines, Carl now washes his feet with rocks.

Entrepreneur Sal Green begins to toy with the idea of starting a cat swimming school.

So much for Jalapeno-flavored perch parts as
a pet food substitute.

"Bad news, Mr. Quigley . . . we've just
learned your interior decorator ran off
with a troupe of gypsies!"

How the brain works.

When choosing a coffee table coaster, select one that might double as a nut dish when you have squirrels over.

Slowly, at first, all three cats began moving up the car's hood toward the windshield.

THIS VEHICLE
MAKES
SUDDEN STOPS

WE
SUPPORT
YOUR
SALES
EXCELLENCE

Manager Fred Barnwall senses a mood shift
among his sales people.

Adrian Barnwhistle is an exception to the adage, "You never forget how to ride a bike!"

"You're gonna spoil that dog, Annie!"

You can just about see where farmer Artie Mason first noticed the bear.

"As you can see, Arnie, the rest of the family isn't that interested in having you back!"

Ex-big-leaguer Alvin (Lanky) Larson has never really gotten his heart into his new career.

Ruth would never have agreed to spend a month tied to Hector had she known he lurched so when he walked.

Lionel the Beagle doesn't particularly care for his new clear plastic collar with the inlaid glitter.

Edwin Halsey continues to pursue his notion that bread is capable of speech.

For Dick and Ruth Farnhoffer, it all started with an
outrageous increase in the cost of rutabagas two summers ago.

Sid has less need than most to know exactly
where he's going.

Mrs. Luebner has some advice: Be sure
and check the length of your drill bits
before tinkering around the houseboat.

"Wouldn't a good flea powder
be more efficient, Basil?!"

Garbage therapy for dogs.

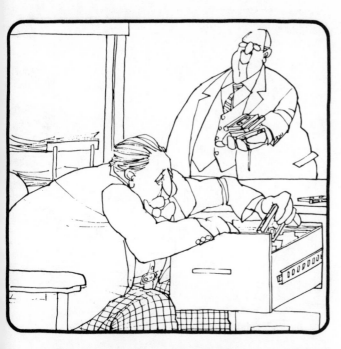

As part of the dismissal process, employees are asked to return their "Up With People" tapes.

"Life is nothing without passion," thought Allen, smugly.

"I rue the day I brought that lamp
into this house! . . ."

David's biological clock fails him again.

"Penny for your thoughts, Arnold!"

Bob is given to occasional acts of dominance.

ASK ME ABOUT
DISARMAMENT

Mr. Bangsiding felt (and wrongly so) that a
little man-to-man chat would be enough to
stop Bob's practical joking.

"Silvan, let's put the dog's worm medicine
downstairs, before someone mistakes it
for mouthwash."

"It's almost like they do it on
purpose, isn't it, Fred?!"

The city fathers hope upon hope that Basil Tweed, architect of the Ear, Nose and Throat Clinic, won't be bidding on the proposed new Proctology Clinic.

"Your pet, Sir! . . ."